AF479827

QUESTIONABLE POEMS

From Beyond the Event Horizon

TERRY SLOAN

Collages by Jon Vickers

Published by Terry Sloan

QUESTIONABLE POEMS

Inside images created by Jon Vickers. Source materials include stills from public domain silent and sound films, public images from NASA and the artist's personal photo albums, all modified, layered and used in the context of fair use.

ISBN 979-8-218-12695-7

Cover photo by Terry Ballard
https://www.flickr.com/photos/terryballard/5137221939

First Printing, 2023

This is the apocryphal origin story of the serendipitous cosmic anomaly that is the book you hold in your hands.

Terry Sloan and Jon Vickers, both life-long cinephiles, struck up a friendship at the Indiana University Cinema where Jon was the founding director. On the road, untethered from the routine of normal life, Terry began spontaneously generating poems, often movie related, which he sent to Jon. In the meantime, Jon retired from the IU Cinema and began producing analog and digital collages to fill a creative void. After Jon had received a critical mass of Terry's poems, he began insisting that something must be done with them. He proposed that some mechanism be found for these poems and images to see the light of day. The result is this book.

I've embarked on a quest for the Ultimate question.
The primal uncertainty that underlies it all.
Warning! Do not operate these poems below abnormal parameters.
Terry Sloan

2 A.M.

Startle in the dark
RUN RUN RUN
Time is short
The end is dear
Cherish
Each pulse of blood to brain
Each fill of lung
Each instance
In the flow of time
Savor the fear
Each clutch of throat
Each heave of chest
Each spasm of bowel
The caul is lifted
And the sightless eyes
Gaze on the face
Of existential angst
Why groan about the present
When it's within your grasp
To manifest the future
And live there

RELENTLESS MEASUREMENT

A Life
Hangs
In the Balance
Onto the Pan
Flows an endless torrent
Orbits of a star
Phases of a moon
Transits of a glowing orb
Ingenuity rears its troubled head
Periods of a pendulum
Cycles of an escapement
Years
Months
Weeks
Days
Hours
Minutes
Seconds
Tenths
Hundredths
Milliseconds
Nanoseconds
Picoseconds
Femtoseconds ...

An Infinity
Of infinitesimal granules
Of Time
What Force to counter this relentless flow
And swing the Scale in my favor?
Gravity?
Heap up all my possessions
Every transaction
Every purchase
Every treasured Thing
Every thoughtlessly discarded item
Every breathe I've breathed
Every tear I've shed
Every shit I've shat
Nothing?
Not a quiver ...

Psychic Energy?
Every difference discerned
Every distinction apprehended
Every instance of beauty appreciated
Every ugliness rejected
Every lover loved
Every enemy hated
Every cruel indifference casually exhibited
Stuck
Immobilized
The Scale won't budge
Not until I vomit forth
The dark, massive bolus
Of my Fear and Despair
Will the pointer quiver
And allow the beginning
Of my ascension

A.I. ART

THIS
Is
Neither
Pipe
Nor
Poem
Nor
Fowl
Nor
NIGHTMARE FISH
Angry Art
Awful Art
Agnostic Art
Abnormal Art
Anatomical Art
Astronomical Art
Anti Art
ALIEN ART ...

First, they came
For your chess players
GO GO OH!
OH the Jeopardy!
Deep Blue
More like Shallow HAL
If Art must spark
An Idea
Or trigger
An Emotion
Who will buy
A false equivalence
Or a crocodile tear
But Art is not commerce
Anymore than Lightning
Is Ones and Zeros

ME ME ME

What can I do?
What can I say?
What can I be?
Less of me

What can I think?
What can I feel?
How do I act?
Like I'm not real

How can I be?
How can I see?
Where do I flee?
Into the Earth
Into the Sea
Into the Air, or
Into the Fire

PUNCH MY TICKET TO THE MARS EXPRESS

Living
In the Land of the Lost
Running
From my past
Shuffling
Toward my Future
Placing
One foot in front of the other
Expecting
A different result each time
Finding
More of the same
Needing
To try a different direction
I choose
UP

CHANCE ENCOUNTER

I met a youthful fellow traveler
Toddling along the table-treed corridors
Of a restaurant wilderness
He pushed before him
A wheeled high chair
Upon which lolled
A six-foot plushly stuffed
Likeness of a snake
I inquired
Is that a boa constrictor?
No, Big Snake
Is that a rattlesnake?
NO, BIG SNAKE!
Does it bite?
No, see his tongue
Acknowledging his confident beatitude ...

I sought his assistance
With my safe passage
For which service
I proffered the offering
Of a single silver coin
As our outstretched hands touched
I saw his eyes widen
Mine following
With the shared joyous realization
That one cannot
Fear the future
In a world
Where a benign indifferent providence
Provides a feckless wanderer
With a snake wrangler
For each Big Snake he encounters

REPORT ON THE HIGHWAY TO HELL

In the division of labor
Among the pillars of civilization
Politicians
Are providing the funding
Scientists
Are improving the pavement
And measuring the progress
With ever greater precision
Religious leaders
Are trying to send someone else
Philosophers
Are ensuring every
Race
Gender
Age
And Body Type
Has an equitable place in line
I guess it's up to
Artists
To turn this damn procession
AROUND

JUST A JUGGALO

What the hell are you looking at?
NO!
What the hell am I looking at!
My face
Facing out into the world
Covered beneath its paint
Declares
My mind
My heart
My station
My philosophy
My music
My grievance
My pain
My rage
My Rejection
My JOY
What does the banality of your visage cloak?

FIGHT OR FLIGHT

Any Glitch away the wind belows
Tangles my toes
Nobody knows
Nobody's nose
Any Direction the clouds hang
Causes Reason to bang
Everyone sees
Everything seize
Anywhere riven the Thoughts flow
Questions I prose
Darken the Knight
Extinguish the Lite
Better stand tight

GET OVER IT

Nature versus Nurture
Is Structure Stricture?
Haiku
Piling impossibility
On top of difficulty
Seek to Form
Carbon into Diamond
Thru compression
My Spirit moves
To the Ecstatic
Beat
Beat
BEATS
My nature craves the heaviest elements
Formed in the exploding core
Of Super Novae
But stop a moment to consider
Do I really want to blow up
Another idea
No matter how inconsequential
Just to see what comes out?
Hell Yeah!

FASTER MOTORCYCLE REQUIRED

I've got the Black Hole Blues
My Mind
My Soul
My Tank
Is half empty
And mostly wasted
And my poetry sucks
At the Least
Less
Than the Void
I throw it into
Fill It Up
In vino veritas
In beer beatitude
In cannabis conundrums
In Speed unspooling
Of the Gordian Not?
Praise be to Allah!
Thanks to the Buddha for Being!
Hep me Jesus!
The lord got ready
An I gots to move
On down the Road
Into the uncertain Future

MIRROR ARE
CLOSER

20
SPECIAL

DISTANCE DIVIDED BY TIME

Speed
Combines
Two great mysteries
SPACE and TIME
Be here now
Rather
Be THERE now
Fast exists
Only relative to
Too Fast
Outrunning light
Is too slow for me
Space exists
Only relative to
Too Far
The dark side of the Moon
Is too near to me
Time exists
Only relative to
Too Late
Do it now

STAR SPIN

Spun Up
I want to know!
My Mind
spins
The Earth
spins
The Sun
spins
Every point of Light
In the night sky
Spins
Magnitude
How fast?
Fattened bands of Light
Offer clues
Time dependence
Faster or Slower?
Immortality seems dubious
And Man's record keeping
Is so fragile
My mind spins
Will we ever know?
Spun Up

QUANTUM DILEMMA

All there IS
Are quantum fields
Particles
Merely fluctuations
Forces
Just couplings
An effervescent foam
Of particles
Popping into
And out of
Existence
But what is a field?
Just a number
For every point in Space
Wherever that IS
And Time
Whenever that IS

REALLY?

Clinging tenuously
To Reality
By my fingertips
It feels like someone's
stamping on my hands
I'd open my eyes and look
But I'm afraid
He looks an awful lot like me

WATCH OUT BELOW!

Rolling stoned
Oscillating
Around a Local Minimum
Fell thru the bottom of
A Potential Well
No Direction Unknown
Spirit moves the Natural World
But my Spirit is troubled
Will moves the Unnatural World
But my Will is paralyzed
Absolute Zero
Seems Imminent

THOUGHTS ON (the film) PERSONAL SHOPPER

Lingering Death
Twined Sex
Hermaphrodite Whole
Shorn of my Maleness
Hollowed Out
Half my Traitor Heart stilled
Am I even Here
Or am I There
Soul riven in Twain
Grasping my Phantom
Appendage
And coming up empty handed

ODE TO (the film) PATERSON

If words
in the mind
are electrical impulses
And words
in the air
are molecular vibrations
And words
on the page
are ink on acid-free paper
How can you equate poetry with permanence
The dog ate my homework
Anyway it was barely there
to start with
If you're untalented
garbage in dogshit out
If you're unlucky
poetry in dogshit out
But everybody knows
You gotta scrape the shit right off your shoes
Then again
in this mostly imperfect
of all possible worlds
How many people will even see
Jarmusch's movie
Those that matter
Or those that don't

YANK THAT DOOR OPEN!

Tired
Of waiting
For GODot
I want
To see
What Ahab saw
The Prime Mover
Beneath the mask
Of Reality
To see
What Van Gogh painted
The continuous effervescence
Of probabilistic Quantum fields
Underlying it all
How to uncloud
My vision
So I can see
To step
Into that VOID

ENTROPY

Outbound
For elsewhen
During
An iterative
Triangulation
Of
A mid-course
Correction
Unable to remember
The future
Attempting
To alter
The past
Asymptotically
Approaching
Escape
I inadvertently
Activated
AUTO-RETURN

JUSTIFYING GUILLERMO DEL TORO

Solid form
Shaping water
Liquid embrace
How yielding
Sliding envelopment
How fearless
To open
Herself
To
Fin
And
Scale
And
Claw

IT COMES AT NIGHT (inspired by the film)

Risk averse
Cling to life
Seatbelt
Car seat
Airbag
Hand sanitizer
SPF 50
Gluten free
EpiPen
Put a bicycle helmet on that kid!
What won't you burn
To keep the darkness at bay?
Some strangers?
Your family?
Your soul?
Struggling to escape
The rot outside
You fuel the rot inside
Don't you see?
It's futile!
Too Late!

MOJAVE

Gone to the Desert
To search for God
Guess he isn't home
But even an agnostic
Can feel
The Devil's hot breath
On the back of his neck
Crazy to run
When all your Demons are internal
Better to bring a gun
And when you've used
Every bullet but one
Save it for yourself

ENDING SCHRÖDINGER'S CAT

Fortune favors the bold
Discovery favors the prepared
Science seeks the unknown
Art pursues the unknowable
But what am i to do
When anywhichwaythewindblows
Follows MY nose
Those selecting
An Arbitrary Direction
Might just as well
Follow me
We're
Lagging behind
Because a direction
Is only
Arbitrary
Before
It's selected
Like SCHRÖDINGER'S Cat

www.ingramcontent.com/pod-product-compliance
Lightning Source LLC
Chambersburg PA
CBHW042050100726
47973CB00014B/206

* 9 7 9 8 2 1 8 1 2 6 9 5 7 *